LITERATURE CONNECTIONS
SOURCEBOOK

Johnny Tremain

and Related Readings

McDougal Littell
A HOUGHTON MIFFLIN COMPANY
Evanston, Illinois   Boston   Dallas

Copyright © 1997 by McDougal Littell Inc. All rights reserved.

Permission is hereby granted to teachers to reprint or photocopy in classroom quantities the pages or sheets in this work that carry a McDougal Littell copyright notice. These pages are designed to be reproduced by teachers for use in their classes with accompanying McDougal Littell material, provided each copy made shows the copyright notice. Such copies may not be sold, and further distribution is expressly prohibited. Except as authorized above, prior written permission must be obtained from McDougal Littell Inc. to reproduce or transmit this work or portions thereof in any other form or by any other electronic or mechanical means, including any information storage or retrieval system, unless expressly permitted by federal copyright law. Address inquiries to Manager, Rights and Permissions, McDougal Littell Inc., P.O. Box 1667, Evanston, IL 60204.

ISBN 0-395-78369-0

Table of Contents

Parts of the SourceBook 2
Overview Chart 3
Customizing Instruction 4

Into the Literature: *Creating Context*

Johnny Tremain 5
Historical Fiction 5
Point of View 5
Forbes's Life 6
Forbes on Forbes 7
Critic's Corner 8
Literary Concept: Historical Fiction 9
Literary Concept: Plot 10
Literary Concept: Point of View 11
Motivating Activities 12

Through the Literature: *Developing Understanding*

Johnny Tremain Discussion Starters 13–16
Related Readings Discussion Starters 17–20
   "The Die Is Cast" 17
   "Monday, March 5, 1770: Who Was to Blame?" 17
   "Children Have Always Worked" 18
   from *The Silversmiths* 18
   "Envy" 19
   "The Fate of the Loyalists" 19
   "Concord Hymn" 20
Reproducible Pages for Students 21
   FYI: *Johnny Tremain* 22–27
   FYI: "The Die Is Cast" 28
   FYI: "Monday, March 5, 1770: Who Was to Blame?" 29
   FYI: "Children Have Always Worked" 30
   FYI: from *The Silversmiths* 31
   FYI: "The Fate of the Loyalists" 32–33
   FYI: "Concord Hymn" 34
   FYI: Glossary 35–36
   Strategic Reading 1–4 37–40
   Literary Concept 1–3 41–43

Beyond the Literature: *Synthesizing Ideas*

Culminating Writing Assignments 44
Multimodal Activities 45–46
Cross-Curricular Projects 47–49
Suggestions for Assessment 50
Test 51–52
Test Answer Key 53–55
Additional Resources 56–58

Parts of the SourceBook

- Table of Contents
- Overview Chart
- Customizing Instruction

Into the Literature: CREATING CONTEXT

- **Cultural/Historical/Author Background**
- **Critic's Corner** Excerpts from literary criticism about *Johnny Tremain*
- **Literary Concepts**
- **Motivating Activities**

Through the Literature: DEVELOPING UNDERSTANDING

- **Discussion Starters** Questions for the class to respond to orally after reading each section, including a Literary Concept question and a Writing Prompt
- **FYI Pages for Students** Reproducible masters that offer students background, vocabulary help, and connections to the modern world as they read the literature
- **Glossary** Reproducible two-page glossary of difficult words for student use from each section of *Johnny Tremain*
- **Strategic Reading worksheets** Reproducible masters to help students keep track of the plot as they read. (Literal and inferential reading)
- **Literary Concept worksheets** Reproducible masters to help students understand the use of literary elements such as theme (Critical reading)

Beyond the Literature: SYNTHESIZING IDEAS

- **Culminating Writing Assignments** Exploratory, research, and literary analysis topics for writing, covering both the main work and the related readings
- **Multimodal Activities** Suggestions for short-term projects; some are cross-curricular.
- **Cross-Curricular Projects** Suggestions for long-term, cross-curricular, cooperative learning projects
- **Suggestions for Assessment**
- **Test, Answer Key** Essay and short-answer test on *Johnny Tremain* and related readings; answer key
- **Additional Resources** Additional readings for students (coded by difficulty level) and teachers, as well as bibliographic information about commercially available technology

Links to The Language of Literature

Connections can easily be made between *Johnny Tremain* and **Unit 4, Part 1, So Much at Stake** in *The Language of Literature,* grade 8.

Overview Chart

	PAGES FOR TEACHER'S USE	PAGES FOR STUDENT'S USE
Literature Connections	**SourceBook**	**Reproducible Pages**
Johnny Trémain	Customizing Instruction, p. 4 Into the Literature: Creating Context, pp. 5–7 Critic's Corner, p. 8 Literary Concept: Historical Fiction, p. 9 Literary Concept: Plot, p. 10 Literary Concept: Point of View, p. 11 Motivating Activities, p. 12	FYI, pp. 22–23
Johnny Tremain Section 1, Chapters I–III, pp. 1–75	Discussion Starters, p. 13	FYI, p. 24 Glossary, p. 35 Strategic Reading 1, p. 37
Johnny Tremain Section 2, Chapters IV–VI, pp. 76–150	Discussion Starters, p. 14	FYI, p. 25 Glossary, pp. 35–36 Strategic Reading 2, p. 38 Literary Concept 1, p. 41
Johnny Tremain Section 3, Chapters VII–IX, pp. 151–233	Discussion Starters, p. 15	FYI, p. 26 Glossary, p. 36 Strategic Reading 3, p. 39 Literary Concept 2, p. 42
Johnny Tremain Section 4, Chapters X–XII, pp. 234–296	Discussion Starters, p. 16	FYI, p. 27 Glossary, p. 36 Strategic Reading 4, p. 40 Literary Concept 3, p. 43
"The Die Is Cast," pp. 298–299	Discussion Starters, p. 17	FYI, p. 28
"Monday, March 5, 1770: Who Was to Blame?," pp. 300–304	Discussion Starters, p. 17	FYI, p. 29
"Children Have Always Worked," pp. 305–314	Discussion Starters, p. 18	FYI, p. 30
from *The Silversmiths*, pp. 315–318	Discussion Starters, p. 18	FYI, p. 31
"Envy," pp. 319–320	Discussion Starters, p. 19	
"The Fate of the Loyalists," pp. 321–327	Discussion Starters, p. 19	FYI, pp. 32–33
"Concord Hymn," p. 328	Discussion Starters, p. 20	FYI, p. 34
	Culminating Writing Assignments, p. 44 Multimodal Activities, pp. 45–46 Cross-Curricular Projects, pp. 47–49 Suggestions for Assessment, p. 50 Test, Answer Key, pp. 51–55 Additional Resources, pp. 56–58	

Additional writing support for students can be found in CommonSpace.

Customizing Instruction

Less Proficient Students

- Prepare students by having them discuss what they know about the American Revolution. Ask them to find portraits of Revolutionary figures they have learned about and to jot down as captions a quotation or statement by or about each person. Post the pictures in the classroom and discuss each person's contributions to the Revolutionary effort.
- Have students listen to the audiocassette version of *Johnny Tremain* as they read. (See **Additional Resources** for more information.)
- Make sure that students understand the fictional nature of the book—that it interweaves fictional characters and events with real people and actual events from history. Although the author has based many of the real people's thoughts and conversations on her research and knowledge of their attitudes and actions, their dialogue and thoughts remain the product of the author's imagination.
- To help with literal comprehension of the book, have students use **Strategic Reading** 1–4 worksheets, pages 37–40, as they read.

Students Acquiring English

- Pair SAE students with English-proficient students who can help them with unfamiliar vocabulary and historical information about Revolutionary times. Make sure students understand that Whigs were patriots eager to revolt from England and that Tories were loyalists, loyal to England. Also, explain the roles of King George and Parliament in English government and what a colony was.
- To help students appreciate the historical significance of events in the novel, encourage them to make connections between these events and similar events in the history of their countries of origin.
- Use the suggestions for Less Proficient Readers listed above.

Gifted and Talented Students

- Students can create a time line and add events as they read. They can fill in with additional historical events when they finish the book.
- Share the Critic's Corner literary reviews with students and have them find other literary criticisms of Esther Forbes's work. Encourage students to discuss these reviews in small groups and write about them.
- Have students choose a specific category of words such as Adjectives Describing People, Household Words, Political or Military Terms, or Technology, and as they read, fill in charts like the one below:

Technology	Meaning in novel	Modern Equivalent
chaise	two-wheeled carriage that the Lytes drive	expensive sports car for two

4 Literature Connections

Into the Literature
CREATING CONTEXT

Johnny Tremain

While researching her 1942 biography of Paul Revere, Esther Forbes became intrigued by the role of trade apprentices in the Revolutionary effort and decided to write a fictional work about them. Her extensive notes for that research inspired many details, scenes, and characters in *Johnny Tremain,* which was one of only two books that Forbes wrote especially for children.

Set in Boston at the beginning of the American Revolution, the book brings to life the adventures of a teenage boy and his involvement with famous patriots like John Hancock, John and Samuel Adams, James Otis, and Paul Revere. First published in 1943, the book has taken its place in the library of memorable historical novels. A testament to Esther Forbes's conviction that children can appreciate mature writing, the book was awarded the Newbery Medal in 1944 for most distinguished contribution of the year to children's literature. In 1957, it was made into a movie by Walt Disney.

Historical Fiction

An example of historical fiction, *Johnny Tremain* introduces fictional characters who interact with real people of an actual time and place in history. The depictions of the historic figures are based on fact, but the conversations and thoughts attributed to them are the author's creation. Fictional events are intermixed with actual events, as the author brings to life a moment of history and creates for readers an image of the times. Historical figures can also interact with fictional characters to give readers an insight into the major personalities of an era.

Set in Boston from 1773 to 1775, *Johnny Tremain* depicts many events and people—the Boston Tea Party and the battles of Lexington and Concord, Paul Revere and John Hancock—that played an important part in setting the course for American independence.

Point of View

While working on a nonfiction book, Esther Forbes promised herself that sometime she would write a story in which she could "make up anything I wanted as long as I kept it typical of the period. Then I would not know merely what was done but why and how people felt." She fulfilled her wish by creating *Johnny Tremain,* told from the omniscient third-person point of view in which an all-knowing narrator sees into the minds of characters.

Forbes's Life

1891	Born June 28 in Westborough, Massachusetts, to parents with colonial New England ancestry.
1912	Graduates from Bradford Junior College.
1916–18	Attends the University of Wisconsin.
1920–26	Serves as a member of the editorial staff of Houghton Mifflin Company.
1926	Marries Albert Learned Hoskins. Publishes first novel, *O Genteel Lady!*
1928–38	Publishes *A Mirror for Witches, Miss Marrel, Paradise,* and *The General's Lady.*
1933	Divorces Hoskins.
1942	Publishes *Paul Revere and the World He Lived In.*
1942–46	Returns to work at Houghton Mifflin.
1943	Wins Pulitzer Prize for history for her biography of Paul Revere. Publishes *Johnny Tremain.*
1944	Wins John Newbery Medal for *Johnny Tremain.*
1947–59	Publishes *The Boston Book, The Running of the Tide, America's Paul Revere,* and *Rainbow on the Road.*
1967	Dies August 12.
1969	"Come Summer," a musical based on *Rainbow on the Road* and choreographed by Agnes DeMille, opens on Broadway.

Forbes on Forbes

On being omniscient as a novelist—

The historical novelist is like God himself so far as knowing his people is concerned. He knows the people in his book really better than he can actually know any one in life. He knows exactly why they fall in love or can't stand being snubbed. He works from the inside out.

QUOTED IN COMMIRE, ANNE, ED., *SOMETHING ABOUT THE AUTHOR*, VOL. 2. DETROIT: GALE RESEARCH, 1990

On why she wrote her Pulitzer Prize–winning biography—

Esther Forbes said that before beginning *Paul Revere and the World He Lived In* she had been writing a novel about a man who remained neutral during the Revolutionary war:

Then the Nazis attacked Poland, and I was suddenly the most unneutral woman in the world. That destroyed all that I'd been writing about. A person who could stay neutral in war! The character was absurd. But I had a great deal of research completed—that is, my mother had done an enormous amount of research for me, and I'd done a lot—so I wrote of Revere and his world.

QUOTED IN *THE NEW YORK TIMES*, AUGUST 13, 1967

On how she got the inspiration to write *Johnny Tremain*—

[A] horse boy . . . brought word to Paul Revere that the British intended to march out of Boston on the night of the 18th of April in '75. He was employed in a stable near the Province House where General Gage had his headquarters, and he had made friends with the horse boys of the British officers . . . one of them let slip the information that troops were being sent out that very night, and "there would be hell to pay tomorrow." As soon as he could he ran to Paul Revere's North Square house . . . to report what he had found out.

I think it is hard for most writers to say exactly when they get an idea for a certain book, but I had this incident in mind long before I had much else. This little incident teased my mind. I would like to have known more about these two boys. Did they really like each other or not? Were they bright boys or stupid boys?—a hundred things. It struck me, as Henry James once said, as a "perfect little workable thing," the germ virus, nucleus from which a story might grow. But I was still busy on *Paul Revere.* That was not the moment to go off on tangents. But once more I said to myself, "Sometime . . ."

FROM FORBES, ESTHER. "ACCEPTANCE PAPER," *NEWBERY MEDAL BOOKS: 1922–1955.* BOSTON: THE HORN BOOK, INC., 1955.

Critic's Corner

P. A. WHITNEY
Whitney, P. A. *Book Week,* November 28, 1943.

This is Esther Forbes at her brilliant best. She has drawn the character of Johnny with such sympathy and insight that he may well take his place with Jim Hawkins, Huck Finn and other young immortals. And, like the books in which these heroes appear, *Johnny Tremain* is a book for young and old. Youth, particularly, will get from it as live and clear and significant a picture of a great period in American history as has recently been penned.

CHRISTOPHER COLLIER
Collier, Christopher, "Johnny and Sam: Old and New Approaches to the American Revolution." *The Horn Book Magazine,* April 1976.

Johnny Tremain, with its message of ideologically motivated war, is so much the product of World War II that one who grew up in the 1940s must honor its clear one-sidedness. Younger historians, products of the 1960s who are currently busy reviving the Progressive interpretation of a generation ago, would be less tolerant. But without denying its outstanding literary merit, Miss Forbes's presentation of the American Revolution does not pass muster as serious, professional history. Not so much because it is so sharply biased, but because it is so simplistic. Life is not like that—and we may be sure it was not like that two hundred years ago. Such an event as a war involving the three major European nations, with implications for the western power structure for centuries to come, is bound to be a complex matter. To present history in simple, one-sided—almost moralistic—terms, is to teach nothing worth learning and to falsify the past in a way that provides worse than no help in understanding the present or in meeting the future.

ZENA SUTHERLAND AND MAY HILL ARBUTHNOT
Sutherland, Zena, and Arbuthnot, May Hill. *Children and Books,* Seventh Edition. Glenview, Ill: Scott Foresman and Co., 1986.

This book gives no one-sided account of pre-Revolutionary days but makes the colonists and redcoats come alive as histories never seem to. The British, especially, are amazingly human in their forbearance, while the confusion and uncertainty of the colonists are frighteningly real. All the details of the everyday life of the period are expertly woven into the story, never dragged in for themselves.

Literary Concept
HISTORICAL FICTION

Set in Boston from 1773 to 1775, *Johnny Tremain* gives readers an accurate picture of New England colonial life and events leading to the beginning of the Revolutionary War. Imaginary characters, who are the main characters in the novel, interact with real historical figures, and plot conflicts are interwoven with actual historical events. The young apprentice silversmith Johnny Tremain meets Paul Revere, John Hancock, and Samuel Adams and participates with other patriots in the Boston Tea Party.

As an example of **historical fiction**, *Johnny Tremain* has the following characteristics:

- The setting is an actual place and time in history.
- The story is told chronologically.
- Imaginary plot events are interwoven with actual historical events.
- Many of the characters are actual historic figures, and fictional characters interact with these historic figures as the plot unfolds.
- The personalities and basic characteristics of the historic figures are based on research, but the conversations and thoughts attributed to these figures are the author's creation. Their ideas reflect the thinking of the time periods they live in.
- The characters are realistic and face conflicts typical of their times. They have no extraordinary powers and must solve real problems as real humans do.

Presentation Suggestions Help students identify the characteristics of historical fiction as they read. You may wish to remind students that historical fiction is set in an actual time and place in the past and combines imaginary characters and a fictional plot line with actual historic figures and real events. **Literary Concept 1**, page 41, can be used to help students graphically track the elements of historical fiction as they read.

Literary Concept
PLOT

The stage is set for conflict in *Johnny Tremain* when we are introduced to Johnny, a bright young apprentice with an overweening pride and a smart mouth that are certain to get him into trouble. Johnny wastes no time in alienating his fellow apprentice, the slothful Dove. Dove's revenge results in an injury that destroys Johnny's future as a master silversmith. When Johnny seeks other work, he is rebuffed. In desperation, he seeks out his wealthy relatives, who also turn their backs on him. He is finally befriended by a young man who is involved with the patriots. The plot structure continues to develop with a series of conflicts and suspenseful complications, as Johnny has further encounters with his relatives and as his participation in the patriots' efforts increases. The final climax and story resolution come with the death of his friend Rab in the battle of Concord. Johnny has matured and learns that there are things that are worth giving your life for.

Following are some of the plot elements that structure the story:

- the **exposition** that establishes the setting of pre-Revolutionary Boston and introduces the characters in the Lapham household
- the **personal conflicts** caused by Johnny's pride and caustic tongue
- the **historical conflicts** between the patriots and loyalists and between the patriots and the British
- the **complications** resulting from Johnny's injury and the Boston Tea Party
- the **mystery** of Johnny's birthright and the **suspense** about the fate of Rab
- the **climax** as Johnny finally learns the circumstances of his birth and about the death of Rab in the battle of Concord
- the **resolution** as Johnny learns that his injured hand can be repaired and he regains hope for a future as a master silversmith

Presentation Suggestions Remind students that **plot** is the sequence of events in a story. Generally, plots are built around a **conflict**—a problem or struggle between two or more opposing forces. Plot structure consists of exposition, which sets the stage; rising action, which consists of complications as the plot becomes more complex, as characters try to solve conflicts, and as suspense builds; the climax, which is the highest point of interest or suspense; and the resolution, which ties up the loose ends at the conclusion of the story. **Literary Concept 2, page 42,** can be used to help students chart the plot events.

Literary Concept
POINT OF VIEW

Employing the omniscient, or all-knowing, third-person point of view allows the narrator of this story to see into the minds of characters, both fictional and historical. It allows the author to tell us what characters think and feel. She can tell us that John Hancock "was so sure of his own good breeding, he could laugh affectionately at the rich-quick vulgarities of the uncle who had adopted him." A historical perspective also emerges as the author projects her own opinions about historical events and people into the narrative and into the minds and motives of the characters.

Here are examples of Forbes's historical perspective as the omniscient narrator in *Johnny Tremain*:

- The political climate of the time: "the political strife . . . was turning Boston into two armed camps. The Whigs declaring that taxation without representation is tyranny. The Tories believing all differences could be settled with time, patience, and respect for the crown." [Chapter IV]
- The Crown's viewpoint on taxation without representation: "England had . . . gone far in adjusting the grievances of her American colonies. But she insisted upon a small tax on tea. . . . It worked no hardship on the people's pocketbooks . . . The stubborn colonists . . . were insisting they would not be taxed unless they could vote for the men who taxed them." [Chapter VI]

Here are examples of the author's historical perspective reflected in the characters' thoughts and actions:

- The Loyalists' or Tories' attitude toward the rising rebellion: "the semi-secret famous Sons of Liberty, those carefully organized 'mobs' who often took justice into their own hands. . . . They could at will paralyze trade, courts, government. . . . The Laphams had hated such lawless seizure of government." [Chapter IV]
- The character and personality of two historic figures: In a dream, Johnny "had been hard at work … boiling lobsters—he and John Hancock and Sam Adams. The lobsters had men's eyes with long lashes and squirmed and looked up piteously. Hancock would avert his sensitive face to their distress. . . . Sam Adams would rub his palms and chuckle." [Chapter X]

Presentation Suggestions: Remind students that **point of view** refers to the narrative method used in a literary work. It is usually either **first person**, in which a character tells everything in his or her own words, or **third person**, in which events are related by a narrative voice outside the action. If events are related from an **omniscient**, or all-knowing, third-person point of view, the narrator sees into the minds of more than one character. In historical fiction, the author's point of view or interpretation of events often influences the way he or she presents and depicts historic events. As students read, encourage them to look for examples of the author's historical perspective and use of the all-knowing third-person to look into the minds of her characters.
Literary Concept 3, page 43, can be used to help students graphically explore the use of point of view.

Motivating Activities

1. **Tapping Prior Knowledge: The Revolutionary War** Ask students to work in small groups to discuss what they know about the American Revolution. Have them make notes of their discussion so they can share their information with other groups. Encourage students to consider the causes of the war, the attitudes of the colonists, and the position of the British. After the groups have prepared their notes, have a volunteer in each group summarize their discussion so that groups can compare their conclusions. Point out different opinions among the groups on the cause of the war and the attitudes of the colonists and the Crown. Have students consider what accounts for different views about a historic event.

2. **Linking to Today: Citizens in Conflict with Government** Help students explore a contemporary situation in which a group of citizens have come in conflict with government. For example, they might consider groups who refuse to pay income taxes or protestors against U.S. involvement in foreign affairs.

3. **When Is a War Justified?** Have students explore American involvement in wars since the country's inception. They can do some research or simply work from their own knowledge. Have students compare American attitudes toward various wars: World War II, Vietnam, the Korean conflict, Operation Desert Storm, and so forth. After students finish their discussion, have everyone make a list of conditions under which Americans believe war is justified. You can use students' feedback to facilitate a debate, or simply have students read their lists and note that people will always have differing opinions about the circumstances under which war is justified.

4. **The Silversmith** Invite an artist or craftsperson who works with silver to show some of his or her work and to explain the process.

5. **FYI Background** Reproduce and distribute to students FYI pages 22–23, which give background on the American Revolution. You might reproduce and distribute all the FYI pages for the novel at this time for students to refer to as they read the novel.

Through the Literature
DEVELOPING UNDERSTANDING

BEFORE READING

You might want to distribute

 p. 24, Glossary, p. 35
- *Strategic Reading 1, p. 37*

Johnny Tremain

SECTION 1
Chapters I–III

AFTER READING

Discussion Starters

1. Do you like Johnny Tremain as a person so far? Why or why not?
2. What good and bad qualities has Johnny shown so far?
3. Why does Johnny take an immediate liking to Rab?
4. Evaluate Mr. Lapham as a master to his apprentices.

> **CONSIDER**
> ✓ the Bible passages he reads
> ✓ his view of his own ability
> ✓ his behavior toward Johnny before and after the accident

5. **Literary Concept: Suspense** Suspense is the growing tension and excitement caused by the questions raised about what might happen in the plot. What questions are creating suspense so far in the story?
6. Johnny turns down Paul Revere's offer to become his apprentice. What do his decision and the reasons behind it tell you about Johnny?
7. To what could Johnny's apprenticeship be compared today? Think of jobs that require similar kinds of training.

Writing Prompt

Write a **help-wanted advertisement** for a silversmith's apprentice. The ad should list the experience and other qualifications required for the job as well as the duties, hours, and pay.

SourceBook 13

BEFORE READING

You might want to distribute

 p. 25, Glossary, pp. 35–36
- *Strategic Reading 2, p. 38*
- *Literary Concept 1, p. 41*

AFTER READING

Discussion Starters

SECTION 2
Chapters IV—VI

1. How did you react to the account of the Boston Tea Party? Explain.
2. How has Johnny's personality been affected by his association with Rab?
3. Do you think Johnny's association with the Sons of Liberty has been good or bad for him? Explain your answer.
4. Does it surprise you that Mr. Lyte called Johnny a thief and had him jailed? Why or why not?
5. What factors contribute to the charge of robbery against Johnny being dropped?
6. Compare and contrast Lavinia and Cilla and the roles they play in Johnny's life.
7. **Literary Concept: Historical Fiction** In historical fiction, made-up characters interact with real figures from history. What positive and negative impressions are you getting of Sam Adams? Paul Revere? James Otis? John Hancock?
8. Do you think a defiance of the government, such as the Boston Tea Party, would be possible today in our country? Why or why not?

Writing Prompt

Write a **newspaper article** about the Boston Tea Party as a reporter for *The Boston Observer*. Write a second version of the article as a reporter for *The London Times*.

14 Literature Connections

BEFORE READING

You might want to distribute

 p. 26, Glossary, p. 36
- *Strategic Reading 3, p. 39*
- *Literary Concept 2, p. 42*

SECTION 3
Chapters VII—IX

AFTER READING

Discussion Starters

1. Do you think Johnny's reaction to Pumpkin's execution shows cowardice? Explain your answer.
2. How has the silver cup Johnny's mother gave him played an important part in his life?
3. As retribution for the Boston Tea Party, the British blockade the port, causing suffering for the people of Boston. Do you think the Boston Tea Party succeeded according to Sam Adams's plans? Explain your answer.
4. Mrs. Bessie warned the Lytes about the oncoming mob. Do you approve of her action? Why or why not?
5. Compare and contrast Sam Adams and James Otis. How would you describe the relationship between the two men?
6. What does Otis mean when he says, "we fight, we die, for a simple thing. Only that a man can stand up"?
7. What differences do you see between Johnny's and Rab's attitudes toward the British?
8. **Literary Concept: Point of View** This story is told in **third-person omniscient** point of view. In other words, the narrator is not a character but can tell all the characters' thoughts and actions. Do you feel that the narrator is giving a fair presentation of both sides, the British and the colonists' points of view, and those in between? Be specific in your answer.

Writing Prompt

Imagine that you are a British soldier stationed in Boston in 1774. Write a **letter** to your parents in England describing some of your experiences and feelings.

BEFORE READING

You might want to distribute

 p. 27, Glossary, p. 36
- *Strategic Reading 4, p. 40*
- *Literary Concept 3, p. 43*

AFTER READING

Discussion Starters

SECTION 4
Chapters X–XII

1. What was your reaction to the end of the novel?
2. How has Johnny changed by the end of the novel? Give some specific examples.
3. Whom do you consider heroic in this story? Give reasons for your choice or choices.
4. Johnny has a dream in which John Hancock and Sam Adams watch a pot of boiling lobsters. What do the actions of these two men in the dream tell you about what Johnny thinks about them?
5. **Literary Concept: Foreshadowing** Foreshadowing is a writer's use of hints or clues to indicate events that will occur later in the story. What hints create suspense and at the same time foreshadow Rab's injury and death?

   CONSIDER
   - ✓ Rab's leaving for Lexington
   - ✓ Johnny's reaction to news of the Battle of Lexington
   - ✓ Dr. Warren's warning to Johnny

6. How do you think regaining the use of his hand will affect Johnny's life?
7. Did your opinion of Lavinia Lyte change after she admits to Johnny the truth about his heritage? Explain your answer.
8. Give a modern-day example in which a group of people have worked or are working together for a good or just cause. How is your example similar to and different from the patriots' cause?

Writing Prompt

Imagine that you were a participant in or observer of events of the American Revolution in and around Boston. Write **diary entries** for each day from April 15, 1775, to April 19, 1775.

BEFORE READING

You might want to distribute
 p. 28

RELATED READINGS
The Die Is Cast

AFTER READING

Discussion Starters

1. What impression do you get of John Adams from reading this letter? Does it agree with the one projected in *Johnny Tremain*?
2. What does Adams mean when he says, "The sublimity of it charms me!"?
3. How might bankrupting the East India Company help the cause of the patriots?
4. Which events that Adams predicted might result as an aftermath of the Boston Tea Party actually happened?

Writing Prompt

Imagine that you are the captain of one of the ships involved in the Boston Tea Party. Write a **letter** to the owners of the East India Company explaining why you were not able to protect their cargo.

BEFORE READING

You might want to distribute
 p. 29

Monday, March 5, 1770: Who Was to Blame?

AFTER READING

Discussion Starters

1. Who do you think was to blame for the Boston Massacre?
2. Why do you think the incident was labeled a "massacre"? Do you agree with the label? Why or why not?
3. Do you think the trial verdicts for the British soldiers were just? Explain.
4. How do you think John Adams, the defender of the British soldiers, felt about Samuel Adams's use of the incident as a means of propaganda?
5. How does the account of the Boston Massacre in this piece differ from what you have learned about it previously?

Writing Prompt

Suppose you were Sam Adams. Write a **response** to this article.

SourceBook 17

BEFORE READING

You might want to distribute
 p. 30

Children Have Always Worked

AFTER READING

Discussion Starters

1. What is your reaction to the treatment of children in earlier centuries?
2. Based on the essay, how do you think children thought about themselves in those days?
3. Which do you think would be worse—to be an orphaned child living on the streets of London or to be indentured? Explain your answer.
4. Could there be advantages to having an apprentice system today? What disadvantages might there be?
5. How do you think society's views of children have changed over the last 300 years?
6. Consider how Johnny Tremain viewed his apprenticeship to Mr. Lapham. Do his views reflect the attitude of this article? Why or why not?

Writing Prompt

Suppose you are the master of an apprentice. Write a **defense** of your position, explaining why you're doing the apprentice a big favor.

BEFORE READING

You might want to distribute
 p. 31

from The Silversmiths

AFTER READING

Discussion Starters

1. What facts in this article particularly interested you?
2. Why do you think the British did not want colonists to mint coins?
3. Why do you think the silversmith craft is not practiced today the same way it was in colonial times? What might some differences be?

Writing Prompt

Pretend that you are a colonial silversmith. Based on this article, write an **advertisement** for your business, emphasizing the quality and value of your work with silver.

18 Literature Connections

Envy

AFTER READING

Discussion Starters

1. What were your impressions and reactions to this poem?
2. Who would you rather have as a friend—the narrator of the poem or the envied boy? Explain your answer.
3. The poet says "there is somewhere a boy whom I greatly envy." What do you think the poet means by this statement?
4. How would you describe the envied boy?
5. What does the speaker tell you about himself in describing the boy?
6. Do you think Johnny Tremain would identify more with the narrator or with the envied boy? Explain your answer.
7. What does the poem teach about envy?

Writing Prompt

What might the envied boy say to the speaker? Write his **reply** to the poem.

BEFORE READING

You might want to distribute pp. 32–33

The Fate of the Loyalists

AFTER READING

Discussion Starters

1. Did your opinion of the Loyalists change after reading this article? Explain.
2. What is the author's opinion of the treatment of the Loyalists?
3. Do you think the Americans treated the Loyalists fairly? Give reasons for your opinion.
4. Based on what you have learned about the American Revolution so far, do you think that the patriots were 100 percent justified in provoking a war?

Writing Prompt

Based on what you learned from this article, write a **letter** to George Washington from a Loyalist point of view, expressing your feelings about your situation after the war.

BEFORE READING

You might want to distribute p. 34

Concord Hymn

AFTER READING

Discussion Starters

1. What images or lines in the hymn particularly appeal to you? Why?
2. What was the "shot heard round the world"? How was it heard world wide?
3. Do you agree with the poet that it is important to remember the deeds of the dead? Why or why not?
4. This hymn was composed about 60 years after the battle of Concord. Do you think it would have been different in tone if it had been composed a year after the battle? Explain your answer.
5. Would Johnny Tremain agree with the sentiments expressed in this poem? Why or why not?

Writing Prompt

Write a **eulogy** for someone who has died—either someone you know personally or a historical figure. Recall the good they have done for others.

These pages for the students give background, explain references, define vocabulary words, and help students connect the modern world with the world of Johnny Tremain. You can reproduce them and allow students to read them before or while they are reading the works in Literature Connections.

Table of Contents

Background	22–23
Section 1: Chapters I–III	24
Section 2: Chapters IV–VI	25
Section 3: Chapters VII–IX	26
Section 4: Chapters X–XII	27
"The Die Is Cast"	28
"Monday, March 5, 1770"	29
"Children Have Always Worked"	30
from *The Silversmiths*	31
"The Fate of the Loyalists"	32–33
"Concord Hymn"	34
Glossary	35–36

Johnny Tremain

BACKGROUND

WHAT KINDLED THE REBELLION?

The King's New Taxes

King George III

Shortly after the French and Indian War ended in 1763, Great Britain took steps to tighten control over its colonies. It also levied new taxes on American colonists to offset the cost of the war. Among the acts that particularly enraged the colonists were

- **The Sugar Act,** March 1764, which added or increased taxes on foreign imports such as sugar, wine, cloth, and coffee
- **The Stamp Act,** October 1765, which required that written material be printed on a special stamped paper obtained from British tax agents
- **The Townshend Acts,** May 1767, which taxed imports such as paper, glass, paint, lead, and tea
- **The Tea Act,** May 1773, which removed all taxes except the Townshend duty and allowed the East India Company to set a lower price than their American competitors who were smuggling tea in from Holland
- **The Intolerable Acts,** May 1774, which closed the Boston harbor, protected British officials accused of committing offenses while collecting taxes or putting down riots, and revoked most of the colony's rights under the Massachussett's charter.

The Rebels' Reaction

Fearing that they would lose the traditional rights of English subjects, the colonists became alarmed and argued that there should not be taxation without representation. These arguments grew increasingly heated until they exploded into the incidents that set off the first shots at Lexington and Concord. Among the colonists' most important acts of rebellion were

George Washington

- **The Boston Massacre** In September 1768 two British regiments were quartered in the hostile city of Boston. On March 5, 1770, a crowd gathered at the Boston customs house and began jeering and throwing snowballs at them. Tempers flared and the troops fired, killing three men and mortally injuring two others. Although the crowd had provoked the shooting, Samuel Adams saw the "Boston Massacre" as a symbol of British tyranny. For years to come, his speeches, pamphlets, and newspaper articles would remind the colonists of that day and continue to feed the fire of liberty.

- **The Boston Tea Party** The Sons of Liberty organized throughout the colonies against the threat of the East India tea monopoly. In Charleston they locked up the tea in a warehouse; in New York and Philadelphia they made the ships leave without unloading; in Annapolis they burned a ship carrying tea; but in Boston they held a party! Disguised as Native Americans, the Sons of Liberty boarded the ships on December 16, 1773, and dumped the tea into the harbor.

- **Lexington and Concord** People in Massachusetts began preparing for war and the British Parliament declared the colony to be in a state of rebellion. Learning of a weapons store in Concord, General Gage ordered British troops to Lexington and then on to Concord to seize them. Alerted by Paul Revere and William Dawes, who had ridden all night to warn them, 70 armed minutemen faced the British troops on Lexington Green on April 19, 1775. Shots were fired and the colonists retreated. As the British marched back toward Boston, the militia lined up along the sides of the road behind stone walls and trees and attacked again. In the ensuing battle, 247 British and 93 patriots were killed or wounded. The British retreated to Lexington, where they met fresh troops. The American Revolutionary War had begun.

Johnny Tremain

BACKGROUND

They Fanned The Flame...

Faneuil Hall, Boston

Samuel Adams

Called the "Father of the Revolution," nobody could doubt—or prove—Samuel Adams's responsibility for the Boston Tea Party. Before achieving prominence in Boston politics in 1764, Adams had not been a success. His malt business had failed and he had little property. Because he refused to collect taxes from those who could not afford them, he had not been successful as a tax collector, and his overdue collections were used as ammunition by political enemies. Then in May 1764, Adams was named to a committee to instruct representatives of the General Court regarding the Stamp Act, and he drew up the first important document against taxation without representation.

Adams was aware of the importance of public opinion and knew how to create and control it. Thomas Hutchinson, the Royal Governor of Massachusetts, called this Adams's "black art" and accused him of using trained mobs to carry out his purposes.

When Adams, on his way with John Hancock to attend the Second Continental Congress in April 1775, heard the firing of muskets on Lexington Green, he is reported to have exclaimed, "What a glorious morning is this!"

John Hancock

John Hancock was a Boston patriot who, as the president of the Continental Congress, became the first person to sign the Declaration of Independence in 1776. In 1765, Hancock, one of the wealthiest men in Boston, risked his fortune by testing the Stamp Act and sending out his ship to London without the required stamped papers. In 1768, the British seized the *Liberty*, one of Hancock's ships, claiming that he had disobeyed regulations. Enraged citizens rioted, and the British sent in troops to restore order. The Liberty Affair, as it became known, was one of the events that led to the Revolutionary War.

John Adams

John Adams, one of the members of the Observers' Club that is mentioned in the novel, was the cousin of Samuel Adams. After the war, he served as the new nation's first vice president. In 1797, he succeeded George Washington and became the second president of the United States. During his term, Adams faced problems caused by insisting on neutrality during the French Revolution. When he later supported the Alien and Sedition Acts, which many felt violated freedom of speech and the press, Adams lost the support of the Federalist party and the election of 1800. He died at age 90 on July 4, 1826.

Paul Revere

Paul Revere was a master silversmith and leader of the Boston Craftsmen. He was a member of the Sons of Liberty, along with John Hancock, John Adams, and Samuel Adams. Esther Forbes correctly places him at the scene of the Boston Tea Party in 1773.

In 1775, learning that the British forces would march on Lexington and Concord in order to seize the colonists' weapons stores, Joseph Warren asked Paul Revere to warn John Hancock and Samuel Adams, who were living in Lexington. On the night of April 18, 1775, Revere rowed across the Charles River. When he reached the far banks of the river, Revere borrowed a horse and began the famous ride that would be immortalized by Henry Wadsworth Longfellow. Along the way to Lexington, he shouted his warning that the British were on their way. Reaching Lexington, Revere warned Hancock and Adams to leave town and set off to carry the warning to Concord. Revere was captured by a British patrol, who let him go after taking his horse. Revere walked back to Lexington, while Dr. Samuel Prescott rode on to carry the alarm to Concord.

Chapters I–III

SECTION 1

Chapter I
Education in Colonial Boston

Although Mrs. Lapham and her daughters had little education and Johnny Tremain had received his schooling from his mother, Massachusetts had one of the most advanced systems of education in the colonies.

The First Schools The Roxbury Latin School, founded in 1635 by the Puritans, was the first formal school in the colonies. In 1639 the Puritans opened the first college in the colonies—Harvard—in Cambridge, just across the Charles River from Boston. Most people did not attend these formal schools, which were for the privileged and for males only.

Dame Schools Many colonial children attended "Dame Schools," which were often run by widows in their homes. At these schools, children learned how to read and do simple sums. Learning to read the Bible was considered important, but learning to write was not, and many people could not even write their names. Teaching by rote—having students memorize facts—was the accepted method of teaching.

Common Schools In 1647, the general court of Massachusetts ordered every town of 50 or more families to appoint someone to teach all children who reported for schooling. These schools were the first free public education system in America.

Latin Schools After completing the common school, a young girl's formal education was over. Boys could go on to Latin school, where they were prepared for college until about age 15. As the name suggests, much of the school day was spent learning to read, write, and speak Latin.

Beer Before Breakfast!

In Chapter I, we learn that ale was a staple at even a "poor artisan's" breakfast table. It was customary in colonial times for everyone—even the children—to have a mug of beer when they first got out of bed in the morning. More beer was served at breakfast, which was eaten around 10 A.M.

VOCABULARY
Chapters I–II
In the Silversmith Shop

annealing oven	an oven for heating metal in order to strengthen it
bellows	a tool for fanning a fire
cast	to pour metal into a mold and let it harden
crimping iron	a tool used to bend metal into shapes
gauge	a tool for measuring thickness
repouseé	a design in relief made by hammering the underside of metal
smith	a metal worker
soldering iron	a tool used to melt a soft metal that can be used to join two pieces of metal

Chapters IV–VI

SECTION 2

The Fate of James Otis

In 1769, during a struggle with a commissioner over the charges of being a traitor, Otis was struck over the head with a sword and seriously injured. It soon became evident that he had received a permanent brain injury. He began to have fits of madness in which he would break windows and fire his pistol wildly. His erratic behavior is described in *Johnny Tremain*. In 1783, at the age of 58, Otis was struck by lightning and killed.

Chapter VI
The Sons of Liberty

The Sons of Liberty were a group of patriots who were ready to fight for the right to have a say in the government to which they paid taxes. The Sons kept their membership secret because the British considered them to be traitors. One commissioner wrote letters demanding that John Hancock, James Otis and Samuel Adams be arrrested, taken to England, and put on trial for their lives.

Franklin's Press

In 1722, the editor of the *New England Current* was jailed for printing an article criticizing legislators. While the editor was in jail, his 16-year-old apprentice (much like Rab) ran the newspaper. The name of his apprentice was Benjamin Franklin.

Boston in 1775
Using another map of Boston in 1775, can you locate the Boston Commons on the map below?

VOCABULARY

Chapters IV–VI
All Attitude

exuberant	extremely enthusiastic
fatuous	foolish; inane; silly
imperturbable	incapable of being disturbed or upset; calm
obdurate	unmoved by persuasion; unyielding; stubborn
pompous	acting self-important, pretentious

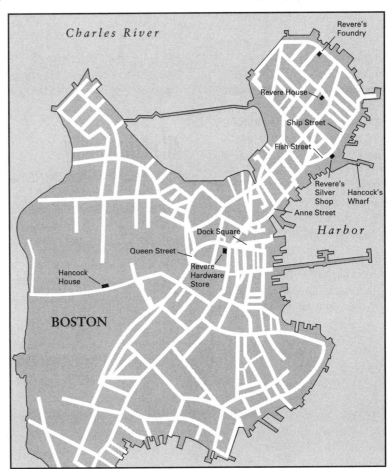

SourceBook 25

Chapters VII–IX

SECTION 3

Chapter IX
James Armistead, African-American Patriot

Both the British and the patriots relied on spies to feed them information. Johnny Tremain is part of the spy network that Paul Revere organized in Boston. During the Revolutionary War, one of the most important American spies was an African-American patriot named James Armistead. Armistead reported to the Marquis de Lafayette, a Frenchman who had volunteered his services to the American effort.

The slave of a Virginia farmer, Armistead went to the camp of Benedict Arnold and volunteered to serve the British officers. Armistead was able to send messages of British plans to Lafayette almost daily. Later he went to the camp of Lord Cornwallis. While serving officers as a waiter at headquarters, he learned, and alerted Lafayette, that the British would be unloading troops at Yorktown.

After the war ended, the slave was granted his freedom in recognition of his services as a spy. He then took the name James Lafayette.

The Daughters of Liberty

Patriotic groups of women, calling themselves Daughters of Liberty, began to organize in 1766, at the same time that the Sons of Liberty began. Recognizing that making their own cloth would allow them to boycott cloth goods from Britain, the Daughters formed spinning groups. Since Britain's major industry was textiles, the boycott would be a serious economic weapon.

The Daughters of Liberty also pledged to give up tea in protest of the Townshend Acts, and experimented with "liberty tea," substitutes made of sassafras, strawberry, and currants.

All in the Family

The wife of Dr. James Warren and sister of James Otis, Mercy Otis Warren was deeply involved in the revolutionary effort. After the Boston Tea Party, John Adams asked Mercy Otis Warren to write a poem about it. The housewife and mother of five children agreed and her poem was published in a Boston newspaper.

Mercy Otis Warren began writing plays that were aired in pamphlet form, since performances were banned in Boston. Her mocking satires of the British delighted the revolutionaries, who passed the printed plays from hand to hand. Her first play, *The Adulateur*, appeared in 1772. In it the Royal Governor Thomas Hutchinson was satirized as a grasping tyrant named Rapatio. She continued to write plays mocking the British and American Loyalists with characters named Brigadier Hate-All, Hum Humbug, Simple Sapling, and Sir Sparrow Spendall.

Chapters X–XII

SECTION 4

LITERARY CONCEPT
Chapter XI

Blending Fact with Fiction

When Esther Forbes was doing research for her biography of Paul Revere she learned that a stable boy had brought word to Revere that the British would march out of Boston on April 18, 1775. The boy had gotten the information from another horse boy who worked for British officers. Forbes worked this historical fact into her novel by having Dove play the part of the stable boy who worked for the British. Johnny is, of course, the other boy.

Chapter XII

Yankee Doodle Dandy

In the novel, the British sing "Yankee Doodle" to provoke the patriots on their way to Concord. The song may have originated in Holland around 1500 as a song sung by harvesters. In England during the time of Shakespeare, it was sung as a nursery rhyme. In the 1600s the lyrics were rewritten to make fun of Oliver Cromwell when he rode to Canterbury to take charge of Puritan forces.

> Yankee Doodle came to town
> Upon a Kentish pony,
> He stuck a feather in his cap
> And called it macaroni.

The term *macaroni* refered to young men fond of wearing unusual Italian clothes

A British army surgeon named Dr. Richard Schuckburgh wrote the words known in the United States. They were intended to make fun of the untrained American troops during the French and Indian War. The troops, however, liked the song and started singing it themselves. The song was sung so often during the retreat of the British at Concord, General Gage is said to have exclaimed, "I hope I shall never hear that tune again!"

Father and I went down to camp,
Along with Captain Goodwin,
And there we saw the men and boys,
As thick as hasty puddin'.

(chorus)
Yankee Doodle keep it up,
Yankee Doodle dandy,
Mind the music and the step,
And with the girls be handy.

And there was Captain Washington,
Upon a slapping stallion
And giving orders to his men,
I guess there was a million.

And then the feathers on his hat,
They looked so 'tarnal finy
I wanted peskely to get,
To give to my Jemina.

And then they had a swamping gun,
As big as a log of maple,
On a deuced little cart,
A load for father's cattle.

VOCABULARY

Chapters X–XI

You're in the Army Now!

artillery horses	horses that pull mounted guns or cannons
billeted	housed or lodged in military quarters
brigade	a military unit consisting of two or more regiments
company	a small group of soldiers
evolutions	military drills; a pattern of repeated movements
light infantry	foot soldiers who carried light arms, often sent to the front on scouting missions
militia	a group of civilians enrolled for military service during emergencies only
regiment	a military unit consisting of two or more battalions

The Die Is Cast

BY JOHN ADAMS

Another Viewpoint

Ann Hulton, a Loyalist and the sister of the Boston commissioner of customs, wrote to a friend in England six weeks after the Boston Tea Party. She described some of the violence that occurred. Following is an excerpt from her letter.

> But the most shocking cruelty was exercised a few nights ago upon a poor old man, a customs inspector named Malcom. A quarrel was picked with him. He was afterwards taken and tarred and feathered.... He was stripped stark naked, one of the severest cold nights this winter, his body covered all over with tar, then with feathers, his arm dislocated in tearing off his clothes. He was dragged in a cart with thousands attending, some beating him with clubs and knocking him out of the cart, then in again. They gave him several severe whippings, at different parts of the town. This spectacle of horror and sportive cruelty was exhibited for about five hours.

An Eyewitness Report of the Boston Tea Party

A man was curious when he heard a commotion outside of Faneuil Hall, a meeting house near the Boston wharves. He went out to see what was happening that night of December 16, 1773. Following is his eyewitness description:

> [Men were mustering] to the number of two hundred. They proceeded two by two to Griffin's wharf, where . . . before nine o'clock in the evening every chest from on board the three vessels was knocked to pieces and flung over the sides. They say the actors were Indians from Narragansett. Whether they were or not, to a transient observer they appeared as such, being cloathed in Blankets with the heads muffled, and copper color'd countenances, being each armed with a hatchet or axe and pair of pistols.

John Adams, a Man of Justice

Although he was a leader in opposing British colonial policies, Adams's sense of justice caused him to defend the officer and soldiers charged with manslaughter in the Boston Massacre. He felt that because they had been obeying orders, the military men deserved to be set free. He worried that his position on the incident would cost him his popularity. Instead, it increased his prestige, and the people of Boston elected him as a representative in the colonial legislature.

Monday, March 5, 1770: Who Was to Blame?

BY JOHN M. BRESNAHAN, JR.

An Atmosphere of Hostility

The Boston Massacre was the result of a series of events that led to increasing hostilities between the loyalists and the patriots. Early in 1770, a 12-year-old boy was heckling a merchant who had refused the Sons of Liberty's demands to not sell British goods. A man who lived nearby and who was an informer for tax commissioners shot and killed the boy. Although resentful of the British troops' presence in Boston, the citizens had put up with them until this incident. The boy's death fired the people's tempers, and they now demanded that the soldiers, who had been quartered in Boston to protect the commissioners, be sent home.

Several months later, a fight began between soldiers and some men led by Samuel Gray, the owner of a rope factory. The soldiers, who were severely beaten, vowed they would seek revenge. This increasing hostility between patriots and British troops set the stage for the violence that would erupt during the Boston Massacre.

Modern Connections

Incidents of political violence such as the Boston Massacre are not uncommon today. In the 1960s, several students participating in an antiwar demonstration protesting the U.S. presence in Vietnam were killed by National Guardsmen. This incident at Kent State University caused growing participation in the antiwar movement. In the 1990s, a group of Los Angeles police officers were tried for beating an African American named Rodney King, who had been stopped for drunk driving. The entire country had witnessed the brutality of the beating when a videotape of the incident was shown repeatedly on national television news shows. When the police officers were acquitted, angry citizens rioted in east Los Angeles.

Crispus Attucks

Crispus Attucks, the first victim of the Boston Massacre, was a slave. The son of an African father and a Native American mother, Attucks was able to earn money for himself as a trader of horses and cattle. But when he wasn't allowed to buy his freedom, Attucks ran away from his master. On October 2, 1750, his master ran an advertisement offering a reward of ten pounds for the return of Attucks. It is thought that Attucks spent many years working as a sailor on cargo ships or whaling ships. In 1770 he was the first man killed in the Boston Massacre.

The Slave in the American Revolution

Although many of the New England colonies had laws that prohibited the "Negro, Indian, or Mulatto" from fighting in colonial armed forces, African-American freemen as well as slaves were involved in the revolutionary effort. A freeman named Salem Poor fought in the battle of Bunker Hill. Several African-Americans fought at Lexington and Concord, including Peter Salem, who is memorialized by a monument in Framingham, Massachusetts. Slaves joined the army because a substitution system allowed a drafted man to get someone else to serve in his place. This opened the door for slaves to earn freedom in exchange for military service.

Children Have Always Worked

BY MILTON MELTZER

Background

Milton Meltzer was born and raised in Worcester, Massachusetts. His interest in history and some of the shocking deeds people have done in its course was first awakened in September 1930 when he was a high school junior. On the day the Nazis came to power shouting "Germany awake! Jew perish!" he says he began to see that what happened in the world could have a devastating effect on ordinary people like himself.

Since then, Meltzer has written more than 80 books for teenage and adult readers. *Cheap Raw Material,* the book from which this selection was taken, begins with the story of children being sold into slavery more than 2000 years ago and ends with a report on children working today.

Meltzer says that one of his reasons for writing is "to expand our knowledge of our own human nature to understand why people were infected by Nazism" and other poisons such as slavery. Books may not solve our biggest problems, but they are a crucial beginning: "However inadequate words are, human language is all we have to reach across barriers to understanding."

Still Working

Until recently, the sale of children as slaves or cheap labor was legal. The United States did not pass laws against employing children under age 14 until 1938. Great Britain, one of the first countries to protect the rights of children, didn't pass its child protection laws until 1884.

Young children are still overworked and mistreated in some parts of the world. Rug and clothes manufacturers in southeast Asia have been discovered forcing children as young as six to weave rugs and cut and sew sportswear in crowded factories for 12 to 16 hours a day.

No Kidding

By 1724, the word *kid,* once slang for a talented young thief, also meant young indentured servant—a homeless or poor child taken unwillingly to the American colonies to serve a master four or five years.

An Appeal for Freedom

In 1773 slaves in Boston and other towns wrote to Governor Hutchinson protesting that they could never own anything, no matter how hard they worked. Later the slaves of Massachusetts asked for one day a week in which they could work for themselves in order to save money and return to freedom in Africa. The governor refused their pleas. However, at the close of the revolution, the Northern states began to free all slaves.

What's the Difference?

Legally, the difference between an indentured servant and an apprentice was important. While both were under contract to work between four and twenty years, the apprentice was supposed to be taught a craft or trade such as silverworking, while the indentured servant got no special training. (In fact, the word *apprentice* comes from the Old French for learning.) In practice, however, both apprentices and indentured servants were subject to the whims of masters. Some indentured servants were taught skills; some apprentices were ignored or mistreated, and both were sometimes denied legal rights and, like slaves, kept in service for their lifetimes.

from The Silversmiths

BY LEONARD EVERETT FISHER

Paul Revere

Famous for his "midnight ride" and fine silversmith craftsmanship, Paul Revere had many other talents.

- He was a successful political cartoonist, even though his drawing talent wasn't great.
- He was a successful dentist and made false teeth from ivory, sheep's teeth, and hippopotamus tusks. The teeth were fastened in with silver wire.
- During the Revolutionary War, he made cannons and gun powder.
- He designed and engraved the copper plates for the first issue of Continental paper money.
- He designed the official colonial seal.
- He opened a successful hardware store in 1783 to supplement his income as a silversmith.
- He set up a copper mill and was the first American to use a process for rolling copper into thin sheathing. The copper sheathing used for the bottom of the warship the *Constitution*, the dome of the Boston statehouse, and the boiler on Robert Fulton's steamship were all Paul Revere's work.

How the Colonists Made Silver

Proud of being apprenticed to a silversmith, Johnny used to look down on the boys who worked at other trades because he felt his craft was superior. Of course, Johnny tended to be a little conceited. However, turning silver into fine cups and plates did take hard work, endurance, and skill.

Because the colonists hadn't started mining silver in America yet, silversmiths had to get their silver from coins. That meant melting coins in shallow pans over extraordinarily high heat to separate the silver from other metals. After repeating this procedure three or four times, they had to mix it with copper, getting as close to the true standard—75 parts of copper to 925 parts of silver—or best quality of silver possible. They then poured the silver into a mold and stored it in bricks called ingots until they were ready to use it.

Making a fine plate or sugar bowl was a whole other procedure. First, the smith had to fire the ingot until it was red hot; then he hammered it, cooled it, and reheated it many times until the silver was leaf-thin. Measuring the drawing of the plate, he cut a circle of silver to the exact size needed; engraved it to mark the center, and began the exacting craft of tapping it, heating it, and tapping it again until he achieved the size and shape required. Only then could he polish the work and add decoration such as the handles Johnny was making for the sugar bowl.

All that Glitters is Not Gold—or Silver

Coins may were the main source of silver in the colonies, but you won't find any silver at all in the coins minted today. The United States stopped putting silver in coins in the early 1970s. It was the last large nation to stop.

The United States still produces about 20 percent of all silver mined in the Western Hemisphere. The medal for producing the largest supply of silver in the world goes to India.

The Fate of the Loyalists

BY CLORINDA CLARKE

Background

"The Fate of the Loyalists" is from a book called *The American Revolution: A British View*. In a note to the reader, the author explains that she wrote the book "to tell English boys and girls about our Revolution." She also maintains that she tried to give both sides of the story. As you read, see if she fulfills her goal—or whether, as the subtitle suggests, the book favors the King's supporters. You might also compare what she says to the way the Loyalists are described in an American textbook.

Our First Civil War

After the Declaration of Independence was signed, every colonist had to choose between supporting the Revolutionary government or Britain. It is estimated that a third were Loyalists, or Tories, who chose to remain loyal to Britain; one third were patriots, or Whigs, who chose independence; and one third remained neutral. Because the choosing of sides tore apart friends, neighbors, and families, some people have said that the Revolution was as much a civil war as a war with Britain.

Loyalists were called betrayers of their country as early as 1774. The Continental Congress called on "committees of safety" to report on their actions, and states adopted laws to punish Tories. The Tories did prove to be a danger. They spied for the British and furnished them with food and supplies. Thousands joined the British in fighting against Washington's forces.

VOCABULARY

Acts of War

confiscate	to take away, usually as a penalty
despotism	rule by absolute power; tyranny
exile	someone forced to live away from the home country
negotiation	a means of reaching an argument through discussion
reprisal	an act of revenge
restoration	the return of a person, object or institution; also refers to the return of the English monarchy in 1660 after it had been abolished for 11 years
skirmish	a fight between a small number of soldiers
vassalage	the state of being a servant, sometimes involuntarily

The Fate of the Loyalists (continued)

The King's Fate

Many Englishmen and women blamed King George III for letting the Revolutionary War go on too long. The unpopular war was destroying the British economy and its military reputation.

King George was criticized even more for the scandalous behavior and corruption of his ministers between 1779–1782. Finally, when a group of young politicians appointed new ministers without even consulting him, George was so humiliated he considered giving up the throne. He got through the crisis by aligning himself with a shrewd politician named William Pitt. But continuing attacks on his leadership left the king badly shaken and the throne weakened. During the next two decades, he suffered a tremendous loss of power, the rebellion of his sons, and excruciating episodes of mental illness. In 1811, he was declared unfit to rule by reason of insanity. He lived his last nine years in isolation with his wife, enjoying only bouts of sanity.

Gilbert Charles Stuart

When you picture George Washington, the image that comes to mind is apt to be the one you've seen in a portrait painted by Gilbert Stuart. Stuart was born near Newport, Rhode Island, in 1755. In 1775 he went to London, perhaps to escape the scorn that he and fellow Loyalists received from the patriots. He opened a portrait studio in London and was very successful, but he lived extravagantly and was heavily in debt when he returned to the United States in 1793. It's ironic that this Loyalist planned to make money by painting the portrait of George Washington, the commander who led the troops against the British.

John Singleton Copley

John Singleton Copley was another Loyalist who was also a well-known portrait painter. Born in Boston in 1738, he sent a painting to a London exhibition. Famous painters praised his painting and recommended that Copley study in Europe. Because he was having success in America, Copley did not go to London until 1774, when he settled there permanently.

Concord Hymn
BY RALPH WALDO EMERSON

Ralph Waldo Emerson

Ralph Waldo Emerson was born on May 25, 1803, in Boston. After graduating from Harvard as class poet in 1821, Emerson began teaching in a finishing school for young women. When the school closed in 1825, Emerson became a Unitarian minister. Finding the church rituals too confining, he broke with the church and went abroad in 1832. He returned in 1833 and settled in Concord, Massachusetts.

His first wife having died some years earlier, Emerson married for a second time in 1835. He and his wife Lydia had four children. His son Waldo died in 1842, and Emerson wrote one of his finest poems, "Threnody," in his son's memory. But he is best known as one of the founders of a philosophical movement called Transcendentalism, which he introduced in his book *Nature* (1836).

In 1837 Emerson gave an address at Harvard titled "The American Scholar." In this famous address he urged people to learn from life, know the past through books, and express themselves through action. By the time he died in 1880, he had transformed American thinking and influenced philosophers throughout the world.

The Hymn

Emerson was asked to write the words to "Concord Hymn" for the unveiling of the monument honoring the beginning of the Revolutionary War. The monument, a simple stone obelisk or column, marks the place where colonial Minutemen battled British troops in 1775. The hymn was sung at a Fourth of July 1837 memorial service celebrating the event. A phrase from Emerson's hymn, "the shot heard round the world," soon became an emblem of the American Revolution and the experiment in democracy that the battle launched.

VOCABULARY

In Honor of Concord

redeem	recall or deliver from neglect
rude	simply built
shaft	column
sires	fathers
votive	offered in honor and thanks

No Ordinary Town

In addition to being the site of the first Revolutionary skirmish, Concord, Massachusetts, has several other claims to fame. During the 19th century, it was home to such famous writers as Ralph Waldo Emerson, Henry David Thoreau, Nathaniel Hawthorne, and Louisa May Alcott and gave birth to the American Transcendental movement. It is also the birthplace of the Concord grape, developed by an agriculturist name Ephraim Bull. Concord still looks and feels like an early American village; many of the writers' homes have been preserved and are open to the public, as are the battlefield and Walden Pond.

Another Monument

In 1875, an up and coming young sculptor named Daniel Chester French (1850–1931) was asked to design another monument for Concord in honor of the war's first centennial. The result was "The Minute Man," a bronze statue that became a symbol of American patriotism on savings bonds, posters, and stamps. French went on to create some of the best-known monuments in the country, including the Lincoln Memorial in Washington, D.C., a statue of Ulysses S. Grant in Philadelphia, and a statue of Ralph Waldo Emerson in Concord, Massachusetts.

Glossary
JOHNNY TREMAIN

Section 1: Chapters I–III

apoplectic (ăp′ə-plĕk′tĭk): *adj.* having apoplexy; prone to a sudden loss of body function resulting from loss of blood to the brain   *p. 9*

arrogance* (ăr′ə-gəns): *n.* a haughtiness, a superior manner   *p. 57*

august (ô-gŭst′): *adj.* inspiring reverence or awe; grand   *p. 20*

autocratic* (ô′tə-krăt′ĭk): *adj.* like an absolute ruler   *p. 6*

brackish (brăk′ĭsh): *adj.* salty or briny   *p. 6*

cooper (kōō′pər): *v.* to make barrels   *p. 46*

crucible (krōō′sə-bəl): *n.* a container used for heating metals to high temperatures   *p. 11*

draft (drăft): *n.* a device for controlling the flow of air in a furnace or oven   *p. 39*

ethereal* (ĭ-thîr′ē-əl): *adj.* light; airy   *p. 6*

flaccid* (flăk′sĭd): *adj.* soft and limp   *p. 53*

johnnycake (jŏn′ē-kāk): *n.* a fried bread made from cornmeal and milk; often called "journey cake" because travelers would pack it to eat on a trip   *p. 53*

laudanum (lôd′n-əm): *n.* a medicinal preparation that contains opium   *p. 42*

mantua (măn′chōō-ə): *n.* a woman's loose gown   *p. 65*

mark (märk): *n.* a symbol identifying the maker of an object   *p. 19*

parasitic* (păr′ə-sĭt′ĭk): *adj.* like an organism that lives on a plant or animal from which it gets its nutrients   *p. 6*

poultice (pōl′tĭs): *n.* a soft mass of moist cloth, bread, meal, or herbs applied hot to the body for medicinal purposes   *p. 42*

rakish* (rā′kĭsh): *adj.* smart; jaunty; dashing   *p. 62*

shunt (shŭnt): *v.* to shift or divert   *p. 34*

soldering iron (sŏd′ər-ing ī-rən): *n.* a tool used to melt a soft metal that is used to join pieces of metal   *p. 18*

stocks (stŏks): *n.* a device for punishment made of heavy timbers with holes to lock in ankles and wrists   *p. 38*

venerable* (vĕn′ər-ə-bəl): *adj.* worthy of respect, usually because of great age   *p. 11*

wattle (wot′l): *n.* the fleshy lobe hanging down from the throat or chin   *p. 71*

whist (hwĭst): *adj.* quiet; hushed; silent   *p. 30*

yoke (yōk): *n.* a wooden device worn over the shoulder for carrying water pails   *p. 47*

Section 2: Chapters IV–VI

apparition* (ăp′ə-rĭsh′ən): *n.* anything that appears in an unexpected or ghostly way   *p. 86*

atrophy* (ăt′rə-fē): *v.* to waste away from lack of use   *p. 112*

catechism (kăt′ĭ-kĭz′əm): *n.* a book summarizing the principles of a religion, usually in question form and answers   *p. 116*

chaise (shāz): *n.* a two-wheeled carriage for two people   *p. 145*

dun (dŭn): *v.* to repeat requests for payment of a debt   *p. 126*

enigmatical (ĕn′ĭg-măt′ĭ-kəl): *adj.* like a mystery or riddle; baffling; puzzling   *p. 95*

PARTIAL PRONUNCIATION KEY

ă	at, gas	îr	dear, here	th	thing, with
ā	ape, day	ng	sing, anger	th	then, other
ä	father, barn	ŏ	odd, not	ŭ	up, nut
âr	fair, dare	ō	open, road, grow	ûr	fur, earn, bird, worm
ĕ	egg, ten	ô	awful, bought, horse	zh	treasure, garage
ē	evil, see, meal	oi	coin, boy	ə	awake, even, pencil, pilot, focus
hw	white, everywhere	ŏŏ	look, full		
ĭ	inch, fit	ōō	root, glue, through	ər	perform, letter
ī	idle, my, tried	ou	out, cow		

SOUNDS IN FOREIGN WORDS

kh	German ich, auch; Scottish loch	œ	French feu, cœur; German schön	ü	French utile, rue; German grün
N	French entre, bon, fin				

---

* The words followed by asterisks are useful words that you might add to your vocabulary.

SourceBook 35

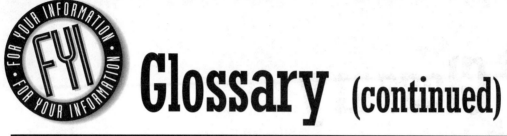

Glossary (continued)

JOHNNY TREMAIN

equitation (ĕk'wĭ-tā'shən): *n.* the art of riding on horseback p. 106

hippogriff (hĭp'ə-grĭf'): *n.* a creature of fables who resembles a griffin but has the body and hind parts of a horse p. 107

palsy (pôl'zē): *n.* an ailment characterized by body tremors p. 124

poke (pōk): *n.* a small bag or sack p. 116

sillabub (sĭl'ə-bŭb): *n.* a drink of cream and wine p. 100

spinet (spĭn'ĭt): *n.* a small upright piano p. 86

surtout : (sər-tōō'): *n.* a man's tight fitting overcoat p. 112

sweetmeat (swēt'mēt): *n.* a cake, candy or pastry p. 116

translucent* (trăns-lōō'sənt): *adj.* permitting light to pass through but dimming it so that objects are not seen clearly p. 82

truckle bed (trŭk'əl bĕd): *n.* a trundle bed; a bed on casters that is stored under another bed p. 140

Section 3: Chapters VII-IX

commandeer (kŏm'ən-dĭr'): *v.* to seize for military or governmental use p. 164

dilatory (dĭl'ə-tôr'ē): *adj.* inclined to delay; slow; tardy p. 229

fraternize* (frăt'ər-nīz'): *v.* to be intimate or friendly with the enemy during war p. 174

gesticulate (jĕ-stĭk'yə-lāt'): *v.* to use gestures in an excited manner p. 152

lascivious (lə-sĭv'ē-əs): *adj.* lewd; wanton; arousing sexual desire p. 178

lassitude (lăs'ĭ-tōōd'): *n.* a state or feeling of being tired and sluggish p. 230

lucid* (lōō'sĭd): *adj.* clearheaded; rational p. 204

militia* (mə-lĭsh'ə): *n* a group of civilians enrolled for military service only in emergencies p. 159

oblivious* (ə-blĭv'ē-əs): *adj.* unaware of p. 155

oratory* (ôr'ə-tôr'ē): *n.* the art of speechmaking p. 158

piqued (pēkt): *adj.* resentful at being slighted p. 199

placate* (plā'kāt'): *v.* to stop from being angry; to calm or make satisfied p. 205

sedition (sĭ-dĭ'shən): *n.* a stirring up of dissatisfaction, or rebellion against the government in power p. 153

toothsome (tōōth'səm): *adj.* desirable; sexually alluring p. 175

wraiths (rāths): *n.* ghosts p. 191

Section 4: Chapters X-XII

enmity* (ĕn'mĭ-tē): *n.* bitter attitude or feelings; hostility; hatred p. 216

evolution (ĕv'ə-lōō'shən): *n.* a military drill; a pattern of repeated movements p. 234

grenadier (grĕn'ə-dîr'): *n.* a foot soldier specially selected for strength and courage p. 234

heretic* (hĕr'ĭ-tĭk): *n.* a person who does not conform to the established view p. 270

pied (pīd): *adj.* spilled; mixed up p. 262

protégée* (prō'tə-zhā'): *n.* a person under the care or patronage of another p. 268

punctilious* (pŭngk-tĭl'ē-əs): *adj.* strict in the observance of rules or formalities p. 246

* The words followed by asterisks are useful words that you might add to your vocabulary.

Name _____

Strategic Reading

SECTION 1, CHAPTERS I–III

Characterization

Characterization refers to the techniques a writer uses to develop characters. One way that a writer can influence your opinion of a character is by a description of him or her. Another way is through the character's words and actions.

In the second column below, indicate whether you think you are meant to like the character. Fill in the other two columns with details that support your answer. The first one is done for you as an example.

Character's name	Are you meant to like this character?	Narrator's description of the character	The character's words and actions
DOVE	yes/**no**	whitish, flaccid, parasitic	He stays in bed as long as he can and works as little as possible.
MR. LAPHAM	yes/no		
MRS. LAPHAM	yes/no		
CILLA	yes/no		
ISANNAH	yes/no		
PAUL REVERE	yes/no		
RAB	yes/no		

SourceBook 37

Name _____

Strategic Reading 2
SECTION 2, CHAPTERS IV–VI

Expectations vs. Reality

Characters and readers alike expect certain things to happen based on what they know. Often events turn out differently from those expectations. In Chapter IV, which is divided into smaller sections, Johnny puts high expectations on the cup his mother gave him. As you read each section, jot down the difference between the characters expectations and what actually happens.

Chapter IV, Section 1 What does Johnny expect to happen when he *tells* Merchant Lyte about his cup?
_____
_____

What actually happens? _____
_____

Chapter IV, Section 2 What does Johnny expect to happen when he *shows* Merchant Lyte his cup?
_____
_____

What actually happens? _____
_____

Chapter IV, Section 4 What does Merchant Lyte expect to happen in court?
_____
_____

What actually happens? _____
_____

Chapter V, Section 1 What does Johnny expect to happen when he returns to Merchant Lyte after the trial?
_____
_____

What actually happens? _____
_____

38 Literature Connections

Name _____

Strategic Reading 3
SECTION 3, CHAPTERS VII–IX

Identifying Cause and Effect

Events in novels are linked by cause and effect. The **cause** in the event that happens first in time. The **effect** is what happens as a result of that first event. One effect can become the cause of another effect. The following chart lists some events described in *Johnny Tremain*. Fill in the chart to show the cause or effect of each event.

	Cause	Effect
1		the Boston Tea Party
2	the Boston Tea Party	
3	Goblin throws Lieutenant Strange, who had commandeered Johnny's horse.	
4	Johnny finds a family Bible in the Lyte's house.	
5		Pumpkin faces the firing squad.
6	Pumpkin faces the firing squad.	

SourceBook 39

Name _____

Strategic Reading
SECTION 4, CHAPTERS X–XII

Noticing Details

Read Chapter X. Then complete the missing diary entries for the historical events described in the chapter.

Day	Date	Historical Event
Friday		British spies return to London.
Saturday	April 15	
	April 16	
Tuesday	April 18	British troops drill.
Wednesday		

Read Chapters XI and XII. Then list at least five things that Johnny must do before he can get out of Boston.

_____
_____
_____
_____
_____

40 Literature Connections

Literary Concept 1

HISTORICAL FICTION

Name _____

Some of the events in *Johnny Tremain* that involve historic figures are fictional, and some are events that actually occurred in history. For each of the historic figures listed below, list the fictional events in the novel that include that figure. Then list the actual historic events from the novel that include that figure.

Historic Figure	Fictional Events	Historic Events
John Hancock		
Paul Revere		
Samuel Adams		
John Adams		
General Gage		

Name _____

Literary Concept 2

PLOT

Fill out the following chart with the main plot events of the novel. Record what happens to Johnny in the second column. Record what happens in the struggle between the British and the patriots in the fourth column. The first event is filled in for you.

Chapter	What Happens to Johnny	Date	What Happens Between the British and Patriots
Chapter I	Johnny begins a typical day in the silversmith shop where he is an apprentice.	June 1773	John Hancock and Sam Adams are speaking out against England.
Chapter II		July 1773	
		August 1773	
Chapter III		September 1773	
Chapter VI		December 1774	
Chapter VII		June 1774	
Chapter IX		Fall 1774	
Chapter X		April 1775	

42 Literature Connections

Name _____

Literary Concept 3
POINT OF VIEW

The author of *Johnny Tremain* uses **omniscient third-person** narration, which means that the narrator is not a character in the story (third person) and can present the thoughts of any character (omniscient, or all-knowing). Thus she can give us insight on Whigs, who are pro-Revolution; Tories, who are pro-British; and characters who are neutral, or undecided. For each character below, circle his or her political beliefs. Then give examples from the novel that support your choice.

Character	Point of View	Examples from Novel
Johnny	Whig / Tory / Neutral	
Mr. Lapham	Whig / Tory / Neutral	
Cilla	Whig / Tory / Neutral	
Mr. Lyte	Whig / Tory / Neutral	
Rab	Whig / Tory / Neutral	
Dove	Whig / Tory / Neutral	
Pumpkin	Whig / Tory / Neutral	

SourceBook 43

Beyond the Literature
SYNTHESIZING IDEAS

Culminating Writing Assignments

EXPLORATORY WRITING

1. Imagine that you are Johnny at Rab's funeral. Write a **eulogy** that Johnny might deliver. The tone and style of the eulogy should reflect the personality of Johnny. The content should describe the qualities of Rab and what he meant to Johnny.

2. Write an **editorial** in which you attempt to persuade your readers of the rightness—or wrongness—of the Boston Tea Party. Support your views with modern-day examples of actions that you see as similar, such as the destruction of private property in the Los Angeles riots of 1992, the bombing of the Federal building in Oklahoma City in 1995, or the refusal of citizens to pay taxes on moral or philosophical grounds.

3. Imagine that Johnny is applying for work at the end of the novel. As if you were Johnny, write a **letter** to your prospective employer, explaining your education and experience and why you are the right person for the job.

RESEARCH

1. Choose one historical figure who plays a part in the novel about whom you would like to know more. Research that person and write a **biographical sketch** about him.

2. Research to find out more about one of the historical events mentioned in the novel. Write a **research paper** about that event.

LITERARY ANALYSIS

1. Write an **essay** that explores the ways in which Johnny has changed and grown through the hardships he suffered and the events he experienced during the war.

2. Christopher Collier accuses Esther Forbes of presenting a one-sided account of the American Revolution. He says:

    > To present history in simple, one-sided—almost moralistic—terms, is to teach nothing worth learning and to falsify the past in a way that provides worse than no help in understanding the present or in meeting the future.

    Write an **essay** in which you agree or disagree with Collier. Support your opinion with evidence from the novel.

3. Write a **comparison** between *Johnny Tremain* and one of the related readings in this book. Compare the fictional treatment in *Johnny Tremain* with the nonfiction treatment of the same subject.

For writing instruction in specific modes, have students use the Writing Coach in the **CommonSpace** program.

Multimodal Activities

Creative Cartography

Suggest that students make a **map** based on locations and routes mentioned in the novel. For example, they might map Boston locations, such as the Common, Paul Revere's house, Old North Church, and Hancock's wharf; the route that Johnny took when delivering papers; or the British troop movements toward Lexington.

Umm, Umm, Good!

Encourage students to research **recipes** for the foods mentioned in the novel, such as johnnycake, as well as other colonial dishes. They might enjoy preparing some of the recipes for classmates to sample.

Make Your Mark

Invite students who make craft items to design a **mark**, similar to a silversmith's, to identify their creations. Students might also enjoy designing a **family crest** that incorporates a motto, such as that of the Lytes. Students whose families are involved in trades could design a **shop sign**.

The Town Crier

Colonial villages had a **town crier** who paraded through the streets ringing a bell and shouting out whatever news he had. Have students pick the events from one day in the novel and relate them as a town crier might.

Revolutionary Scenes

Invite students with artistic ability to draw **battle scenes** at Lexington and Concord, using in part the descriptions in the novel as a guide. They can alternatively take different scenes of Boston described by Forbes and draw them.

Military Music

Have students find a **recording** of "Yankee Doodle" and play it for the class. Invite them to compare it to other military or fighting songs (for example, "John Brown's Body" or "Battle Hymn of the Republic"). They can find recordings of these as well. Ask students to discuss the roles that such songs play in building morale in times of war.

SourceBook 45

Colonial Job Fair

Have students research the jobs Johnny considers, rejects, or is refused—or other jobs that Johnny doesn't even think of. Then they can stage a colonial **job fair.** Students might work individually or in pairs, giving oral presentations about the jobs.

No, but I Read the Book

Show students a videotape of the movie *Johnny Tremain* (see Additional Resources, page 62) and then have them **discuss** how the movie compares with the novel. Encourage students to notice which scenes from the novel are omitted in the movie, which scenes have been added, whether the movie is faithful to the spirit of the novel, and whether the characters in the movie are as they imagined them while reading the novel. Students can also list plot variations between the two versions in a chart like the one below and give their opinions about the merits of those variations.

Johnny Tremain, The Novel		*Johnny Tremain,* The Movie	
Main Events	Characters	Main Events	Characters

I Read It in the Funnies

Ask students to create a **political cartoon** about one of the incidents in *Johnny Tremain* or in the related readings. Encourage students to do different versions of the cartoon, one from the Tory or British point of view and one from the patriot point of view.

Cross-Curricular Projects

The Boston Observer

Overview:

In this project, students will publish an issue of *The Boston Observer* for any week they choose, from 1773 through 1775. Their task is to work cooperatively to design the format of the paper, write and edit the articles, create political cartoons and other illustrations, write advertisements, set the type, and print and distribute the paper.

Cross-Curricular Connection: Journalism, Art, History

Suggested Procedure

1. Have students define the tasks required to complete the project and then form groups to work on tasks according to their interest.

2. Have students zero in on one specific week in their research, attempting to recreate specific news of that week. Remind them that they can report on events not only in Boston but in other parts of the Colonies or in the world beyond them. Suggest that students write their articles as if they were living at that time and observing what they describe.

3. When designing the format of the newspaper, encourage students to research to find a typical page size and typefaces of the times. (If you plan to use a copying machine to make multiple copies, caution students to work with a page size that fits their reproduction method.)

4. If students do not have access to computers and desktop publishing software, encourage them to come as close as they can to the newspaper "look" of colonial times using calligraphy, a typewriter, or any other tools available to them.

5. When their paper is complete and printed, invite students to take copies home to share with family and friends and to distribute copies to other students in their school.

Teaching Tip

Encourage students to submit for publication in *The Boston Observer* previous projects that they have completed. Many advertisements, recipes, editorials, eulogies, and political cartoons created for Multimodal Activities and Writing Prompt assignments will be appropriate for the newspaper.

You Are There

Overview:

In this project, groups of students will choose a scene from the novel that they think would make an interesting dramatization. Each group will perform their scene before the class.

Cross-Curricular Connections: Art, Drama, Film, Music

Suggested Procedure:

1. Divide students into small groups. Have group members choose a scene they would like to dramatize.
2. Have the groups write and rehearse their scripts.
3. Suggest that groups consider enhancing their performance with costumes, props, set design, and music.
4. When students are ready to stage their performances, they should perform them for the class. If the setting of a scene is outdoors, some groups may prefer to videotape their scenes in a park or on the school grounds.

> **Teaching Tip**
>
> Allow students to obtain help from other groups if they require a large number of actor "extras" for their scene.

A Colonial Banquet

Overview:

In this project, students will research recipes typical of colonial times and prepare some dishes for a class tasting or lunch.

Cross-Curricular Connections: Social Studies, Home Economics

Suggested Procedure:

1. Divide students into groups and ask them to research colonial recipes.
2. After students have completed their research, create a master list of all the different dishes. Have each group select one dish to prepare. Negotiate so that each group prepares a different item.
3. If there are accessible kitchen facilities at your school, arrange time for the students to use them for their food preparation. If there are no facilities available, encourage volunteers to prepare the recipes at home and bring them to school on the day selected for your tasting.
4. Have a colonial lunch or snack-tasting party.
5. Encourage students to compile their recipes into a cookbook.

> **Teaching Tip**
>
> You might want to combine the tasting party with presentation of another project.

48   Literature Connections

Survivalists

Overview:

In this project, students will debate the issue:

If alive today, Samuel Adams would be a member of the survivalist movement.

Cross-Curricular Connections: Social Studies

Suggested Procedure:

1. Begin this project by having a class discussion of the survivalist movement. Have students share what they know about the movement. Ask questions to prompt the information that survivalists do not believe in paying taxes and believe that the Federal government has too much control and is usurping individual rights that are guaranteed by the U.S. Constitution.
2. Have students form small groups and perform research on the survivalist movement and on Samuel Adams in preparation for their debates.
3. Let each group decide which side of the debate they wish to argue. However, if a disproportionate number of groups choose one side, you may have to negotiate with some groups to change sides.
4. Each group should select one member to present their argument in debate with another group. You can match the teams for debate by drawing lots.
5. After each debate, have the audience vote for the winner—the debater who presented the most persuasive argument.

> **Teaching Tip**
>
> You might prefer to have students debate on the topic of what political party Sam Adams might lead today, or whether he would be a liberal or conservative rather than survivalist.

Suggestions for Assessment

Negotiated Rubrics

Negotiating rubrics for assessment with students allows them to know before they start an assignment what is required and how it will be judged, and gives them additional ownership of the final product. A popular method of negotiating rubrics is for the teacher and students individually to list the qualities that the final product should contain, then compare the teacher-generated list with the student-generated list and together decide on a compromise.

Portfolio Building

Remind students that they have many choices of types of assignments to select for their portfolios. Among these are the following:

- Culminating Writing Assignments (page 44)
- Writing Prompts, found in the Discussion Starters
- Multimodal Activities (pages 45–46)
- Cross-Curricular Projects (pages 47–49)

Suggest that students use some of the following questions as criteria in selecting which pieces to include in their portfolios.

- Which shows my clearest thinking about the literature?
- Which is or could become most complete?
- Which shows a type of work not presently included in my portfolio?
- Which am I proudest of?

Remind students to reflect on the pieces they choose and to attach a note explaining why they included each and how they would evaluate it.

For suggestions on how to assess portfolios, see **Teacher's Guide to Assessment and Portfolio Use.**

Writing Assessment

The following can be made into formal assignments for evaluation:

- Culminating Writing Assignments (page 49)
- a written analysis of the Critic's Corner literary criticism
- fully developed Writing Prompts from the Discussion Starters

For suggestions about assessing specific kinds of writing, see **The Guide to Writing Assessment** *in the* **Formal Assessment Booklet.**

Alternative Assessment

The following can be used for performance and product assessment.

- Multimodal Activities pages (45–46)
- Cross-Curricular Projects pages (47–49)

Test

The test on pages 51–52 consists of essay and short-answer questions. The answer key follows.

Name _____

Date _____

Test
Johnny Tremain and Related Readings

Essay

Choose two of the following essay questions to answer on your own paper. (25 points each)

1. Do you think that Johnny's injury makes him a stronger and better person? Support your answer with details from the novel.

2. After hearing Lavinia's explanation of his heritage, do you think that Johnny cares about being related to the Lytes? Explain your answer.

3. Do you think that reading this novel would significantly help a person understand the events, people, and social conditions behind the American Revolutionary War? Support your answer with details from the novel.

4. One reviewer criticized *Johnny Tremain* as being too simple and one-sided a presentation of history. What is your opinion of the presentation?

Mark the following scale to show whether you think the novel presents a balanced perspective or whether it favors one side over the other. Then write an essay that supports your opinion, using examples from different parts of the book.

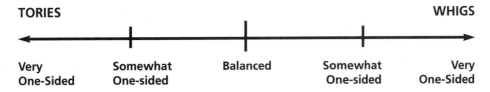

TORIES — Very One-Sided — Somewhat One-sided — Balanced — Somewhat One-sided — Very One-Sided — **WHIGS**

5. Choose one of the following pairs to compare and contrast:

   a. the accounts of the Boston Tea Party in *Johnny Tremain* and "The Die Is Cast"

   b. the explanations of the silversmith's craft in *Johnny Tremain* and in *The Silversmiths*

   c. the depictions of Tories or Loyalists given in *Johnny Tremain* and in "The Fate of the Loyalists"

SourceBook 51

Name

Date

Test (continued)

Johnny Tremain and Related Readings

Short Answer

On your paper, write a short answer to each question below and give a reason for your answer. (5 points each)

1. Why does Johnny agree to take on the order for a sugar basin for John Hancock?
2. What role do you think Johnny's pride plays in his being injured?
3. How does Rab's reaction to Johnny's injury compare to other people's reactions?
4. Do you think Lavinia Lyte was being truthful when she said that her father never meant to trick Johnny out of his silver cup? Why or why not?
5. James Otis and Samuel Adams do not get along with each other. What do you think is the cause of their animosity?
6. Why does Johnny feel guilty about watching Lavinia Lyte from afar?
7. What does Johnny's mastery of riding Goblin tell you about him?
8. Do you think that Johnny's feelings about Merchant Lyte and Dove have changed by the end of the novel? Explain your answer.
9. Which of the following characters do you think would fight so that "a man can stand up": Dove, Cilla, or Lieutenant Stranger?
10. By the end of the novel, do you think that Johnny is as committed to the revolutionary cause as Rab was? Why or why not?

Test Answer Key

Johnny Tremain and Related Readings

Essay

Answers to essay questions will vary, but opinions should be stated clearly and supported by details from the text. Suggestions for points to look for are given below.

1. Most students will feel that Johnny's overcoming his injury does make him a stronger and better person. He becomes more humble, develops a serious interest in the social and political events of the time, is forced to do things that are difficult for him, develops strong loyalties, risks his life for the cause of freedom, and becomes more mature and less impetuous. Students who feel that the injury does not make him a better person will argue that it was not the injury that caused the changes. He would have changed and grown even if he hadn't been injured.

2. Some students will feel that Johnny does still care about being related to the Lytes as evidenced by his great interest in hearing about his relationship to the family. Students who feel he no longer cares will note the great bitterness he has felt toward them. They will also note that the conversation with Lavinia destroys Johnny's strange romantic passion for her.

3. Most students will feel that anyone who reads this novel will gain a significant amount of knowledge about the events, people, and social conditions surrounding the revolutionary conflict. They might note that the novel helps the reader to understand what the situation in the colonies was like for ordinary Americans of the time, how they reacted to British rule, and why so many were willing to risk their lives for independence. Students who do not think the novel increases one's understanding of historic events might argue that most of the events are fictional and the ones that are historical are extremely well-known already.

4. The majority of students will probably state that the novel generally presents a balanced picture of events and attitudes of the times. Both the British and patriot positions are explained, and the British are shown as normal human beings, not warmongers. Although an American reader's sympathies will naturally be for the patriots, the presentation is balanced because Samuel Adams is shown as someone who will manipulate events to get the outcome he desires. Some might feel that the novel gives a lopsided presentation in favor of the Whigs because the one truly evil character, or villain, Merchant Lyte, is a Tory, and all the Whigs are shown in a good light. Few students will feel that the author has gone to extremes to present the British or Tory viewpoints.

5. a. Students might note that *Johnny Tremain* gives a very brief description of the actual event, with much more exposition devoted to events leading to the Tea Party. In "The Die Is Cast" John Adams tells what he thinks the results of the action will be and of his feelings about the action. "The Die Is Cast" is a first-hand account by a real person who really experienced it; whereas the descriptions of events and of people's feelings in *Johnny Tremain*, although based on research, were written by a person far removed from the actual event. Students may note that reading "The Die Is Cast" helped them appreciate the accuracy of the depiction of events and motives in the novel.

b. Students will note that *The Silversmiths* gives a much more thorough explanation of the craft than *Johnny Tremain*. Those details that are given in the novel agree with those in the article. Students should note a difference in author's purpose for the two pieces: The purpose of *The Silversmiths* is to inform. Although the novel does inform the reader about historical events and life of the times, the primary purpose of *Johnny Tremain* is to entertain.

c. In comparing the depictions of Tories in *Johnny Tremain* and "The Fate of the Loyalists" students should comment, among other things, on the different perspectives of the authors, one being American and the other British. Students may feel that "The Fate of the Loyalists" gives a more sympathetic and thorough treatment to the Loyalists.

Short Answer

Answers will vary but should reflect the following ideas.

1. Johnny took on the order for the sugar basin for John Hancock because he was encouraged to by Mrs. Latham and because of his confidence in his ability to tackle a difficult job.

2. Many students will say that Johnny's injury has little to do with pride—it was caused by Dove's deliberately hostile action and bad luck. Others will note that Dove's action was caused by his antagonism toward Johnny, whose pride caused him to belittle Dove. If he hadn't taken pride in his ability to meet a deadline, he wouldn't have rushed and been careless.

3. Rab, unlike other people, virtually ignores Johnny's injury, while other people react with horror, disgust, or pity.

4. Most students will feel that Lavinia was not being truthful because she is characterized as being shallow and deceitful. Or they might feel that although Lavinia may not have been able to face the fact that her father was deceitful, Merchant Lyte was in reality deceitful.

5. James Otis is portrayed as being much more idealistic in his patriotism than Samuel Adams. Adams is rebelling because of taxation without representation. Otis is rebelling for reasons of human dignity, so that a "man can stand up."

6. Johnny is strangely attracted to Lavinia. His guilt may be because she is related to him. He may feel that he is sneaking or spying on her by observing her when she is unaware of being watched.

7. Johnny's ability to ride Goblin, a skittish horse that others are afraid to ride, tells us that he is determined, doesn't give up easily, and is brave.

8. By the end of the novel, Johnny recognizes some of the problems that make Dove and Merchant Lyte act as they do. He no longer hates them, but has come to pity them.

9. From the characteristics they have displayed, Cilla and Lieutenant Stranger would fight for human dignity. Both have displayed honesty and courage. It's doubtful that Dove will ever overcome his cowardice.

10. Even though Johnny has had good relationships with Lieutenant Strange and Pumpkin and obviously doesn't consider all British his enemies, he probably is as committed to the cause as Rab was. His vision is not as narrow as Rab's seemed to be.

Additional Resources

Other Works by Esther Forbes

America's Paul Revere. 1990.
A biography of the great patriot and silversmith, this is the only other book that Esther Forbes wrote expressly for children.

Paul Revere and the World He Lived In. 1942.
This book is the Pulitzer Prize–winning biography of Paul Revere.

FICTION

Avi. *The Fighting Ground,* New York: Harper Trophy, 1987. Thirteen-year-old Jonathan is eager to fight for freedom. As the battle progresses, he learns much about the realities of war and the complexity of justice in this award-winning historical novel. **(average)**

Clapp, Patricia. *I'm Deborah Sampson: A Soldier in the War of the Revolution.* New York: Scholastic, 1977. This historical novel shows readers Johnny Tremain's world from a girl's point of view. **(easy)**

Collier, James Lincoln and Collier, Christopher. *My Brother Sam Is Dead.* NY: Four Winds Press, 1974. This Newbery Honor Book tells the dramatic story of a young boy torn between his Loyalist father and the rebel brother he loves. **(average)**

Fleischman, Paul. *Saturnalia.* New York: Harper and Row, 1990. Saturnalia was a free-wheeling ancient Roman holiday celebrated by masters and slaves exchanging places. The tradition was eventually transported to colonial Boston, the setting of this historical novel. It highlights the lives of a tithingman, a printer, a printer's apprentice, a captured Narraganset Indian, a wigmaker, and the wigmaker's shady servant. **(average)**

Luhrmann, Winifred Bruce. *Only Brave Tomorrows.* Chicago, Houghton Mifflin, 1989. Faith Ralston's genteel life in 17th-century England comes to an abrupt end when her father returns and takes her back to the Massachusetts Bay Colony. Smart and resourceful, Faith gradually learns to adapt. Then war erupts and offers even harder challenges. **(average)**

NONFICTION

Davis, Burke. *Black Heroes of the American Revolution.* San Diego: Harcourt Brace Jovanovich, Publishers, 1976. This book lists the contributions of African Americans to the revolutionary effort, including the earliest martyr, Crispus Attucks, and the master spy James Armistead. **(average)**

De Pauw, Linda Grant. *Founding Mothers: Women of America in the Revolutionary Era.* Boston: Houghton Mifflin Company, 1975. Ladies, servant girls, African-American slave women, and Native American women are included among these profiles of women of the revolutionary era. **(average)**

Fryatt, Norma R. *Faneuil Hall, Cradle of Liberty.* New York: The World Publishing Company, 1970. This book traces the history of Faneuil Hall, Boston's famous meeting house, from its construction to modern times, and includes profiles of the historic figures who entered it. **(challenge)**

Lee, Martin. *Paul Revere: A First Book.* New York: Franklin Watts, 1990. This biography stresses the versatility of the great silversmith. **(easy)**

Lindsey, Clifford. *Colonists for Sale.* New York: Macmillan, 1957. A history of indentured servitude in the colonies. **(easy)**

McDowell, Bart. *The Revolutionary War.* Washington, D.C.: National Geographic Society, 1967. The author tells the story of the Revolutionary War in pictures, including almost 200 paintings and photographs. **(average)**

Meltzer, Milton. *The American Revolutionaries: A History in Their Own Words, 1750–1800.* New York: Thomas Y. Crowell, 1987. Using letters, diaries, journals, memoirs, interviews, ballads, newspapers, pamphlets, and speeches, the book gives eyewitness accounts of events of the revolution. **(challenge)**

Smith, Robert. *The Massachusetts Colony.* London: Crowell-Collier Press, 1969. A history of the colony from the first settlers in the 14th century through August 2, 1776, when it became a commonwealth. **(average)**

Warner, John F. *Colonial American Home Life.* New York: Franklin Watts, 1993. A description of the everyday lives of the colonists—what they ate, their homes, clothing, work, schools, and entertainment. **(easy)**

MULTIMEDIA

American History Video Series: 1. Colonial America in the 1760s (planting the seeds of revolution); *2. Taxation without Representation* (British enforcement and colonial resistance); *3. Prelude to Revolution* (acts of rebellion); *4. Lexington, Concord, and Independence.* Videorecording. Guilford, CT: Media Basics Video. Four of a seven-volume series on the American Revolution. 25 min. each. **(videocassette)**

Johnny Tremain. Dramatized adaptation with music and background sounds. Sundance Publishers. **(audiocassette)**

Johnny Tremain. Self-paced program with 5¼-inch Apple-compatible diskette, backup diskette, users manual, and 16-page study guide. Sundance Publishers. **(computer Software)**

Johnny Tremain. Disney, 1957. Popular film directed by Robert Stevenson and starring Hal Stalmaster, Sebastian Cabot, and Richard Beymer. Color; 80 min. **(videocassette)**

Johnny Tremain. Phonodisc. Newberry Award Records, 1970. A dramatization of the novel. **(phonodisc)**

Johnny Tremain. Sound recording. Prince Frederick, MD: Recorded Books, 1994. An audiorecording of the complete book on seven cassettes. **(audiocassette)**

The Madness of King George. Hallmark Home Entertainment, 1995. A videorecording of the British film about George III. 110 min. **(videocassette)**